Shade and Shelter

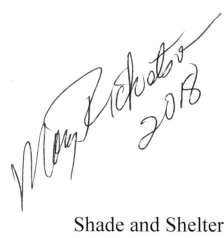

Mary Ricketson 2018 (handwritten signature)

Shade and Shelter

for the broken and the healing

Poems by

Mary Ricketson

*For Cynthia & Roy!
For all the times our
children have shared,
grown into fine men.
Mary* (handwritten inscription)

Kelsay Books

Cover: Photograph by Mary Ricketson

ISBN: 978-1-947465-53-4

Kelsay Books
Aldrich Press
www.kelsaybooks.com

For Lee, the future

Acknowledgments

Grateful acknowledgement is given to the following publications in which these poems and essays originally appeared, some in earlier versions.

Fly With Me, published by *Old Mountain Press:* "How to Rest in the Afternoon"

I Hear the River Call My Name: "Counsel for Myself," "Fear," "Manifesto," "Sunday Seven A.M."

Hanging Dog Creek: "At Leatherwood Falls," "Born to Walk," "Secret Scars," "Stones at Sunset," "Walnut"

It's All Relative: "Homesick"

The Hills Are Alive, published by *Old Mountain Press:* "Unbidden"

They Stood Alone, published by *Old Mountain Press:* "Die Hard"

Wish You Were Here, published by *Old Mountain Press:* "At the Ballet"

Whispers: "Toxic," "Divine Time," "Morsels"

Wild Goose Poetry Review: "The Ritual of Tea," "Shame"

Yin Yang, published by *Old Mountain Press:* "Prophecy"

Poetry in Plain Sight, Winston Salem NC: "Live Today"

"Pure Gold" received gold medal in Silver Arts Medals in the Cherokee County, NC, Senior Games 2015

Special appreciation to Nancy Simpson, 1938–2018,
who believed in me.
And to the Appalachian Mountains that sustain me.

Contents

Part I: Wind

Wild Wind	15
Stones at Sunset	16
Anointed on August 21, 2017	17
Midnight Beans	18
Too Late	19
Die Hard	20
Skip Day	21
Homesick	22
Weather a Change	23
Ghost of the Wood	24
How the World Ticks	25
Cairn	26
The Ritual of Tea	27
Divine Time	28

Part II: Earth

Shade and Shelter	31
Flashback	32
Periphery	33
Fools Gold	34
Prism	35
Trance	36
Midnight	37
Breaking	38
Fighting for Life	39
Wind Dance	40
Breakout	41
Walnut	42
Unbidden	43
Confluence	44

Part III: Moon

Morsels   47
Born to Walk   48
Placing the Sorrow   49
Fear   50
The Danger of Breath   51
Shame   52
Secret Scars   53
Toxic   55
Unquenched   56
Prophecy   57
Prayer for Pardon   58
Excellence   59
Sunday, Seven A.M.   60
Counsel for Myself   61

Part IV: Sun

Silk Patches   65
Secrets   66
Snowed In   67
Fragile Side of Sanity   68
Letters to a Soul Mate   69
Shape Shift   70
Return to Wonder   71
Dance at Last   72
At the Ballet   73
At Leatherwood Falls   74
How to Rest in the Afternoon   75
Love and Adore   76
Live Today   77
Motherless   78
Wedding Toast   79
Perfect Rhythm   80
Manifesto   81
Pure Gold   82

About the Author

Part I: Wind

Wild Wind

That south wind blew,
I loved the start of it.
Snarled hair from end to end,
coat torn off my shoulders,
challenged steps, a feat of balance,
oddly exhilarated, I hurried
from school bus to home.

Later all four winds blow wild,
Medusa my hair, unbalance my step,
wave fear and wreckage across my path.

Wind dips behind dark clouds.
Walnut limbs hold tight, guardians of the night,
wait for rain-start, hold vigil till daylight.

All my memories gather in remembrance
of storms past.
Over and over, exhilaration enters,
rearranges my life,
never to hunger, never to thirst.

Stones at Sunset

I mow around each blueberry bush,
check for fungus, culprit that stole
my crop last year. Later I'll be back,
pull out persistent inner weeds.
Plump green berries
inform me without speaking,
This could be a good year.

By fluke I found this path,
grew beyond my plans.
Familiar now, I did not grow up this way.
Fate steered me in different directions.
My caring hands encourage these berries
to give sustenance and health.

My after supper walk
rhythms my thoughts, calms my mind.
White blooms of blackberries
lead the way, then bursts of daisies
cluster under locust and barbed wire fence.
Three horses almost say hello.

I spy a neighbor's stone wall,
grey and brown random rocks,
dug from a garden one by one,
stacked with no mortar, held together
only by weight and gravity.
In this light, accidental patterns of stones
resemble the chance routine of my life.
Will gravity hold me up so well?

Anointed on August 21, 2017

On the day of days the moon
chewed a bite from the sun
then slipped across its circle of light.

I felt a chill as the sky darkened.
A light breeze took hold.
Evening crickets started a song.
My dog went to bed.

Suddenly the sun
became a halo,
brilliant around the moon.

Then the moon moved left,
began its finale.
Normal seemed to return
but still I sat spellbound,
anointed by the sun.

Now I prize these blades of grass
and dirt beneath my feet.
I learn the ancient language
of sun and moon.

Midnight Beans

These beans
the ones I string and break
by the summer full moon
will taste
good this winter when you come home.

Mindless by now
my fingers go numb.
Time passes slow
on this porch chair as I look
to the sky, brilliant round of light.
But I don't need to see
these beans while I sort and do them up.

I broke up clods
and planted, soon as frost was gone
watched for sprouts, true leaves,
got a good stand,
later pulled weeds, hoed and tilled under strong sun.
I picked at dusk,
cool evening promise of a breeze.

Lap full of beans
now wet from wash,
fingers stroke each bean
one by one,
simple chore in need of time.

This night of beans is empty
but the perfect moon
fills the whole sky.

Too Late

A lone Monarch flies across my garden,
feasts on final drops of nectar, purple salvia.

Hundreds at a glimpse, these regal butterflies
used to swoop, dive, flit back up
in splendid arches, migrate
through my mountains in mid-September,
route to Mexico imprinted by instinct.

Millions die by starvation now, man's inhumanity.
Extinction looms.

Wood cutters, builders, urban-izers
raze the Monarch habitat.

Die Hard

Last buds last petals
of this knock out rose
sit pristine on tall rigid stems
green with thorns that could be nails
flanked by thin oval leaves that could be hand saws
toothed in intricate precision.
Red petals, whatever left in late September,
sit regal, as if the wind will not blow,
as if cold will not bite,
as if the sun will be its friend forever.

Let the breeze rustle up what it will.
I shake like the last leaf in the wind.

Skip Day

Playing hooky from winter,
I bask in fresh air,
let it tingle, brush against bare hands,
stroke exposed arms and elbows.

Sunlight filters through clouds
in a mild, 'Now I see you, now I don't'
kind of way. Down coats, hats
and gloves rest in the closet,
worn out from spells of snow and ice.

Like homework waiting for attention,
that cold nip will come again.
But today a pair of bluebirds play house
and robins fill my field.

Homesick

That tree house, small plank floor
close to the sky, was my home.

I didn't sleep there, eat there,
or do my school work there.

I appeared to have a home eight blocks away,
along with others who shared my name.

Carrying my doll, all of her handmade clothes,
pretend supplies for an imaginary tea party,
I walked, alone or with one friend.

We climbed a rough trunk, hoisted legs over branches,
somersaulted onto an oak platform built by someone
a time before, a time forgotten
until my discovery. I could have landed on the moon
and not been more proud.

I think the sky was blue. I know the leaves were green
then gold. I remember it all was mine for a time.

Weather a Change

These days I write from the dirt, find sprouts,
sprinkle water, wait for sunshine.
These days I take my time, in case the best grows slow.

These days I find a chair just my size, keep a book nearby
and listen to sounds of breeze, rustling leaves.
These days I leave, take a walk, come back
to see what's grown while I've been gone.

These days the grass fails fast in the field, holds on for dear life,
yellow gold, then reddish tinge, then brown like hay.
One spark could set three acres ablaze
then hit the berry farm, next the forest of pine, oak, hickory, poplar.

These days the pond is thirsty even after torrents
of angry rainstorm rage and squall but fill only a thimble.
After this dry earth blots its parched lips on damp air,
that precious water passes by like a traveler on the way to
elsewhere.

These days cold and warm are changelings,
walk in each other's worlds.
Flowers bloom at peculiar times,
rebel like adolescents, change for sake of change.

These days I squirm round and round
like a dog looking for a place to sit,
intent to find a niche.

Ghost of the Wood

In a dense understory, an hour between rains,
one clump of rare Indian Pipe surprises me mid-path
on the well-rotted forest floor.

Atop solitary stems, each white blossom nods,
bows toward the ground,
lush acid loam it calls home.

This single flowered ghost plant accepts food
from fungal hosts hidden deep in dark rich soil,
no chlorophyll desired. Sun peeks through shade.

Mushrooms appear near one majestic hickory.
Fallen leaves fill with raindrops.
One stalk of crimson fire-pink blushes bright.

This forest reveals secrets of dead trees
who drop their limbs piece by piece
next to leaves of trillium past bloom,
maple saplings, and swells of ground pine.
A million ferns hold hope for the future.

How the World Ticks

One woodpecker way down the hollow
pounds familiar questions into a dead oak.

Water spouts from a fragmented drain pipe,
tries to keep a lonely field from flooding.

Creeks flow over pebbles and boulders,
mesmerize with roar, swish, swirl.

Winter was winning
but the wind has changed,
charts a new course.

Nearly dusk, my feet dodge puddles on a gravel path.
Weary, I sort the day, count my wishes as I plod home.

Tired of winter, bored with reality,
I charm the pasture, will it to turn green.

Spring peepers call, predict
warmer days, longer nights.

Almost home, a rising mist draws me deep.
I ponder how the world ticks
and what to do with my one chance.

Cairn

Stacks of stones
along a rutted road,
balance points the way.
A dream inspires, suggests a path
to navigate, connects a map and compass.

The rocks speak, spell a plan for action.

The Ritual of Tea

It starts with a thought,
choice of leaf,
choice of cup, steps to brew,
time to steep.

Sit, sip, taste, until
a familiar rhythm of well-being
stirs some sensuous element
into an ordinary moment.

Let the feeling steep.
Slow is the pace.
Quiet is the way,
last drop a final thought.

Re-tuned,
the end of tea time signals
start of a new hour.
Breath flows easy,
a particle of peace.

Divine Time

A waning moon wiles behind the treetops
down toward Rose Creek, settling time
before the world wakes up.

Days grow short, air crisps, winter looms.
Tall Queen Anne's lace and purple ironweed
grace the field in this darkness.

Here in my divine time,
floundering for a thread of peace
to hold all day long,
I wonder and wait.

What will daylight expose?
Seeds of fortune fall by chance.
What will move into all the spaces
left by falling leaves
and the one who walked away?

Part II: Earth

Shade and Shelter

White Toes lies on the covered porch
of an empty house on a quiet corner.
Tired or weak, he does not speak
his story of escape from dog to dog
aggression, his own home a mile away.
What else happened two months ago?

My Midnight does not spar, does not play,
does not test the waters to connect.
She walks on by. White Toes shrinks into the edges.

Prayers for rain abound, beg for end
of summer's long draught.

No language comforts this canine
who will not return to his pack.
Mysteries of misunderstandings collide
in my raucous thoughts.

Now two humans have turned from each other.
I cannot explain why I shrank away
but I have told him all I know.

The beech tree spreads its broad leafy arms,
welcome embrace of shade and shelter.
I fill plastic bowls with food and water,
set them down by White Toes on my way to town.

Flashback

It was a day when jewelweed necklaced the land.
The first leaves of sumac had turned crimson
and a red shouldered hawk flew
across the only road around.

It was a day for worries to compost,
bubble and ferment, then clean
with tickles of teal tipped butterflies.

It was a day of honeybees but no sting.
Sunlight touched my forehead.
A gentle breeze wrapped
its arms around my waist.

But then, in one second,
all the colors changed.
The sun quit shining.
I blinked,
spiraled half way round to look,
shaking inside.

That red truck drove by.
A glimpse of the man at the wheel
clipped my wings again.
I saw his face and it all came back.

Periphery

It was a time of tight knots.
Fear displaced fun, delight,
and the taste of chocolate cake.

It was a place where Saturday
in the park, sounds of sax and guitar
declined to comfort a worried mind.

It was a day when laughter
could not cover conflict,
caution never soothed an un-named shadow.

It was the kind of trip
that made delayed flights, bumper to bumper traffic
seem the easy way home.

Fools Gold

When I was a fool
I transplanted wild rose,
laid rocks almost slick as mud
on my front walk.

Desperate for beauty,
money scarce,
strangled by transplanted briars,
I should have known better.

When I was a fool,
I held to love,
told myself it would have to do.

Fear dripped from my shoulders,
down my arms and off my fingers.
I squeezed over on my garden bench,
made room for a phoenix to sit beside me.

My heart shook like the last leaf
on a red oak as the wind barrels
with the first killing frost.
From the dust of my life
I discovered how afraid I'd been.

Prism

Nightmares of my life take center stage,
sit on my dresser, put on my shoes, fill my fridge,
walk my path, and mess up my sleep
until I find a light to shine
on one side of me and then another.

In the luminescence I discover a prism.
Reflections sparkle red, orange, yellow,
all the way to violet. A spectrum of colors
pigments my thoughts, dyes my troubles
until the crisis calms.

One by one nightmares shrink,
exit or adapt quietly
to the colors in my prism.

I don't know who to thank,
so *I thank the world,*
a diverse array of friends and strangers,
different colors, varied in language and size.

I thank a circle of humans, animals, and trees
holding hands, a circuit of light,
radiant beam on my prism.

Trance

This clock speaks with two hands,
demands immense attention
on the mantle above.

My life shouts.
Unseen voices pierce my ears.
Unexpected.
Ghosts crowd the shadows,
crouch against the mantle,
demand an ear, insist I remember.

For a minute I don't remember
what I've become.

Midnight

Memory of that black snake in the house
pops up like a charm, reveals a missing link.
I should be sleeping, but I startle
myself from lethargy to full scale alert.
My mental data rearranges,
rapid speed like a Rubix cube
finally falling in place, piece by piece.

Now I know how the snake
got in, and what went wrong with us.

Breaking

That day, I finally knew you.
Everything was your way.

I could charm you left a little,
steer you right a step or two,
almost comfortable in my lead

but you jerked back your stride,
thought I followed,
footstep by footstep.

I was only a mirage,
someone you thought was there,
soft to your touch
but you squeezed harder
and I was gone.

From a distance,
I spy the emptiness that kills you.
I was only real
when you touched me softly
and watched me
outside your normal.

Let the breeze rustle up what it will.
If the limbs of our together
fall from the tree
then let our love turn to rich soil,
feed some other love not yet born.

Fighting for Life

The guise of love
fooled me time after time.
Year after year I fell to the ground
alone but not alone.
Day after day I examined my fingernails,
searched corner garbage dumps
and told stories not my own.

Finally the great owl perched by my porch seat
for nine minutes
one night when the stars did not shine.
I sat frozen for an hour
then stood up,
cleared my eyes, blinked,
turned around three times,
clapped my hands
and let the memory of a rainbow speak to me.
I slept a long sleep
then walked straight into the morning sunrise.

Wind Dance

That day I danced with wind,
let it twirl me gently,
then tango like thunder,
finally fade into the last waltz.

I remembered every wind that set my sails,
every breeze that blew my horn.

I hid from its tornado,
buckled and bristled against
its forced bear hugs and coyote calls,
held my breath till the tempest quit,

then I ran away for rest,
dreamed until cool breezes
softened the heat of summer.

I danced on tiptoe in moonlight,
hoping to make friends with fairies
who know the secrets of this moody lover
called the wind.

Breakout

Helpless, bound by worry,
tethered to tradition,
fettered with a worn out mind.

Want to fly like a bird,
instinct my best map,
food my only need.

Want to break down fences,
light the passions of life,
walk past the end of the trail,
leave the eagles behind
and get on to the sun.

Want to be somewhere
far away, close to safe.

My mountains are burning
and it's hard to find my way.

Walnut

Suddenly I remember
life is hard.

One walnut tree stands
at the end of my field.
Forty years I watch. It never wanders
never moves, only sheds its leaves,
drops its weakest branches
when storms rage through the cove.

What is a woman,
but a tree that walks around?
Storms and seasons leave scars
on ripened beauty,
carve hearts in the bark
where mysteries of strength lie
in the eyes of each beholder.

No decision diverts the tree.
A tree does not worry about its fate.
Straight and tall
it stands
through all seasons.

Unbidden

Wild purslane shows up, center garden
next to snap beans and summer squash.
These dark green turgid leaves
used to be pulled out as weed.
Now I welcome this surprise, this wild friend.
I cultivate around it, tend it well,
along with my extraneous thoughts.

Later I'll eat it raw,
season with salt and lemon juice,
a solstice tonic on this longest day.
I've learned a little
about this weed turned valued food.

I know less about surprise thoughts
that fly in like unexpected seeds.
I tend them too, try not to damage.
One could be a gem,
a glow of color like a prism,
a new facet of light
in the minefields of my mind.

I see your picture in my mind
as I leave the garden,
wonder, my new friend,
if you are precious as you first appear,
a surprise good as purslane.

Confluence

Light a candle in memory
of friends who died.

Still the creeks flow,
Rose Creek into Dockery Creek,
soon to join Hanging Dog Creek.
Smell of fresh-cut pine
fills the quiet roadside air.

Light a candle for the love and friendship,
suddenly found dead by the wayside.

Pick the last mess of beans.
Cut stalks of basil before it's too late.
Red clover and yellow buttercup
still color the pasture in spots, soon to meet
the killing frost.

Light a candle for the bird who lost
its short life at my window.

Clean the house,
cook beans and potatoes,
then rest while rain falls.

Light a candle for the end,
abuse laid to rest by apology
fifty years later.
Heal the pain at break of day.

Part III: Moon

Morsels

Today my fear comes
in a covered dish
disguised with herbs and spices,
made palatable by bits of beef
braised in burgundy,
best features forward.

Starting to love this fear,
I name it Respect,
sprinkle with safety, trust, and hope,
place the casserole in a slow oven.

Fine cuisine, seasoned and cured,
quiets less welcome morsels
of shame and humility.
Integrity rises, meringues the surface,
tempts taste buds past tradition.

Born to Walk

In the dark
hallways where ghosts
of ages lurk, my history
hides and waits.

I prepare myself.
No backpack. No tent.
Only water for the washing.

I was born to walk
where angels do not live,
where invisible demons
lie in wait, pretend to love.

Before I die
my journey will cut down
ancient icons of a time
when eyes were closed
and memories were zipped shut.

What else is there to do?
I must hike a trail
too dark for trees,
too narrow for two.

Placing the Sorrow

Under the beech tree,
beneath a circle of hard cracked dirt
surrounded by lush wild green
beside a rushing creek
three lengths of lonely lie buried.

When the moon is just right
and stars hide from view-
the deer forget to feed
and the owl does not call,
the lonely stirs.

You can hear it shout.
You can feel it stand.
You know the words of its demand.
You quarrel till tree limbs shiver
and silent is an unknown word.

Finally, when lonely tires,
puts down its protest posters
and crawls back underground,
you walk a steady slow pace,
eyes straight ahead,
you bury the feeling
and disappear from the beech tree.

Fear

       walks in,
stares me in the eye
until finally I blink.

Fear gets a toehold.
I hardly know he's here,
so illusive, such a sleuth.

Yesterday he set up camp
while I was unaware.
I thought myself protected,
a guard at every post.

I finished my chores,
sat to rest, to enjoy sunset
and a goodnight kiss.

But fear was in my chair,
on my table, and in my bed,
commanding my attention,
demanding one dance
before I rest.

Now I have no choice.
I know not the tempo
or the time involved.
I submit.

I dance with fear,
my eyes wide open,
looking for his eyes to blink.

The Danger of Breath

You can hear them breathing
like dogs, hot heavy hovering gasps.
They come closer.
I hide, try to shrink smaller.
They get louder.
I begin to shake, the shock
of that beating breath still at bay.
It looms closer by the minute, louder now,
so close the hiding may not hold.
I stop breathing, barely move
for fright of being found.
You can still hear them breathing
like wet dogs on the loose,
ready to latch their teeth to an arm or a leg.
I slink into a crevice,
place I slip and slide
without even knowing,
place where myself hides from me
when danger sets its store.
I escape unseen.
The breath passes on by.

Shame

It was like I spilled deep red spaghetti
on my best white dress,
all down the front
in the middle of people who never knew me,
women and men who by simple human existence
appear important,
definitely privileged to judge me.

I am a spectacle of careless inconsideration,
deplored, lamented, un-forgiven.

I quietly step back, back,
small imperceptible movements.
I fade into invisibility,
oblivion, no words to explain.

Secret Scars

She is smitten
by his first touch.
Already she belongs to him.

Blindfolded,
she does not see
what she surrenders.
His affection feels honest
and secure.

She wants it.
But what seems sincere
might be façade.

She speculates, lost
in a juvenile mind: magic,
clouded cause and effect,
she believes he is her dream.
Euphoria drifts in like a spell.
She is duped, drugged.
Real or imagined
she feels soothed, reassured,
smothered in the attentive arms
of his caress.

She re-enacts childhood,
finds comfort
where comfort
was when life was crazy,
when all the grown ups
wore blindfolds
and no mother's child

could comprehend
the cunning touch
of older hands.

Toxic

Caution. Poison ivy crawls
up straight and steady,
usurps the life of that old poplar tree,
obscures leaves once clear.

Orange jewelweed grows over there,
antidote to poison ivy itch.
Bring me potion to cure my ills,
compress my wounds.

I bleed easy these days.
Words cut like glass.
Cold winds of hate
knock me to my knees.

Unquenched

It's that temper, the dark one, with words
that shoot real bullets straight to the gut,
draw blood red as fire, inflame the tender zones.

That day, life crashed down.
I'm not dead but my heart stopped
and my mind won't work.

Who wants a beating by words,
poison arrows that pierce and paralyze?

Bless the burst.
Bless the tears
Bless the fire still unquenched.

Prophecy

Go away, little girl from the woods,
send back my sweet smiling Mary.

Mother-words meant to shame
when I was rude, talked back,
or fell into deep pensive thought.

When I grew up
I found my home in the woods.
Sun and moon greet me in their own time.
Birds call in the morning, frogs croak at night.
I smile of my own accord.

Prayer for Pardon

Mother to Son

I will say this much.
I never meant to burden you,
obligate you, teach you
such self sacrifice.

These beans grew in bad weather.
Still they feed us. Our home, with all its flaws,
grew you straight and tall.
Marks from storms and foiled plans
have not marred your countenance.

Beware. Some would have you serve,
rescue those who only wait.

Do not be bound
by shackles that are not yours.

Excellence

I told you young, *Reach for the stars*.
Reach higher now, when starlight shines on you.

Time did more than pass. Your keen eye
honed an edge. Desire to learn, discern
became your sword, your grit.

Never settle for predictable.
Roads less taken are your best bet.

Always dream, never run short
of new haunts beyond arm's reach.

Look to the sky every night,
gather light to inform your dreams
before break of day.

Sunday, Seven A.M.

The waning moon
looked graceful
in the eastern sky.
I hardly felt the frigid
wind as I collected wood
to start my parlor fire.

And then the moon
slipped aside, replaced
by red and pink clouds
presiding over last night's
yet un-trodden snow.

In a moment it was over.
I stepped inside, arms full of logs.
But I was warmed before
the fire warmed the room.

Counsel for Myself

I am a place
where people
pilgrimage
the mysteries
of their lives.

I belong to adventure.
I am an anthropology
of psychic alterations
and effervescent lust
looking for life illuminated.

When I feel a storm
coming on
I pick bouquets
of daisies before
it is too late.

I want a silver platter,
exquisite in design,
nothing but the best,
big as my arms can hold.

Bring it to me.
I need to unload my cauldron
of life and death responsibilities,
people with grief and sorrow
who find a home with me.

I need a rest from worry
and surveillance. If I could
free my arms of all I hold,

I would hold myself,
rock myself, dance
until an angel comes
and sings me softly into sleep.

Part IV: Sun

Silk Patches

Pain of old sits on attic shelves
or buried leagues under,
still festers wide open
when wind blows hot and dry.

Clean cut this time,
fresh wounds from the past,
blood red

pain feels new,
slices layers of scars
healed over by time,
desperate need, a will to live.

Turn around quick,
before paralysis sets in
again, before death gets a grip.

Find your old silk coat,
patches sewn on well,
still a perfect fit.
Wear it well,
walk straight into the sun.

Secrets

All pretended no rape, no fist, no bruise, no break.
All kept secrets till one eye opened, then another.
Finally, a shelter emerged, safe place to start again.
Maple trees out front held the red tinge of spring growth.

Old ladies shared stories long held.
Women called crazy told of knives, chains, guns,
slowly unraveled mysteries of shrouded lives,
red blush of innocence long gone.
Fear kept watch on locked doors.

Children came. One hid in the corner,
two told stories, three made cookies,
all prayed their secret prayers.
The maple trees stood in the lush of summer leaf.

Helpers held hands, crafted steps to safety,
stairways to income.
Coworkers unveiled their own secrets,
abuse untold, afraid to know,
afraid of losing love.
The maple trees lost their leaves in winter,
cycled in seasons over and over.

And then we learned it's not so easy
to break the cycle of power and control,
center page of every abuse.

Snowed In

Learning to cook alone,
eat like a queen
and not get fat again.

Today I made two biscuits from scratch,
fractioned the recipe in my head,
stirred and patted to perfection,
waited while my oven did the magic,
ate each delectable buttered bite
and watched single snowflakes
fall peacefully from sky to ground.

Fragile Side of Sanity

Freedom has a hefty price.
Leave all familiar behind.
Take care, safety a premium.

Recently exempt from struggle,
do not knuckle down, do not strain
or make the obvious tangible.

Listen for wisdom when west winds blow.
Watch rain till the last drops fall.
Imagine rays of sunlight.

Expect nothing. Await everything.
Labors of a life unfold within,
new life within the old.

Letters to a Soul Mate

I
In the laboratory of whatever
we are to each other,
I learn nuances of unavailability,
mine and yours.
I hide from myself
more than from you.
I wonder what you see
while I squeeze my eyes tight,
afraid to open.

II
In the silent words of my mind
I talk to you, wait for answers
to questions unasked.
I learn small details
of my own self-protection,
wonder how one iota
of observation could latch
to another, make a sensible thought
worth speaking.

III
Oblivion is comfortable
but bestows no blanket
to keep out the cold
of unspoken desire.

Shape Shift

That day the wind shifted,
well drillers drove to my place,
dug deep into untapped dirt.

Hours passed tense and quiet,
finally water flowed clear and right.
A winter ice storm waited,
almost patient, until all was done.

An hour later grey clouds broke,
pummeled pellets of ice, then a blizzard
slammed snow sideways,
slipped into a two inch snow,
covered every divot and blemish on the ground.

That day safety displaced danger,
wood fire warmed the house.
That night sleep came easy.

That very next day a bluebird returned,
sat on a perch at the circular door
of his unpainted house.
I watched and watched,
struck by brilliant blue
and his rusty red breast.
I marked his return, ready for spring.

Return to Wonder

Late afternoon sun beams
after three days of rain.
Clean white dogwood blossoms
dot the mountain slope.
At my feet a fallen branch
from the cherry tree,
victim of the morning storm.

I follow a gurgling creek, muddy from rain.
This water knows where it's going,
rushes over rocks and logs,
keeps its purpose secret.

Cardinals flit from tree to tree.
Unseen warblers sing to each other.

I am watching for trillium,
petite prize of these mountains.

First I find wild geranium,
then sprouts of wild oats not yet flowered,
and mounds of maidenhair fern.

Finally at the forest edge, I spy my treasured trillium,
short bursts of pink dangle mid three leaves of green.
I slow my pace to see them well, admire and applaud
these wild wonders.

Then I stop, back up for a better look.
Right there, among the trillium,
two pink lady-slippers stand in bloom.
Once I gave up on ever seeing them again.

Dance at Last

I want to die dancing
with a feather in my hat,
a gaudy necklace dangling long
and a smile big as the world.

A jig will suit the scene,
then a reel, sashay down the row
of those who keep on living.
Prance, twirl, keep on dancing.

Never stop the rhythm,
circle of life.

At the Ballet

Sun shines down the mountainside,
reflects eight foot icicles uphill from our trail,
makes a bee line for the tree line
on the mountain top across Woody Gap.

Tall trees with ragged branches rise
graceful as ballet dancers in second position.
Fallen trees, newly snapped or long decayed, conjure a sober mood.
We walk with extra care across the slickest path.

We know these trees by their bark:
hickory, white oak, red oak, poplar.
They speak to us like old friends.

Sapphire blue among striated clouds, the sky is the prize of the day.
Its mood is cold but familiar:
I'll be here long after you leave, it says in reassuring language.
We pass a churchyard on our drive home,
eloquent statement of what remains after leaving.

At Leatherwood Falls

Lost in a world
without words
I linger on a ledge
between brashly
falling waters

waiting for wind
to whisper.

I am delicate now,
almost fragile
like a fine antique
with exquisite patina
that comes only with age.

I wear a *handle with care* label
reserved for rare or expensive goods.
I require time, quiet and attention
to understand my complexity.

I aim to become a prism,
many facets, light shining,
refracted on each surface,
all the colors of the rainbow,
simple, elegant, one of a kind.

How to Rest in the Afternoon

Lie in a hammock
near the house, but away
from everything.
Notice sunlight filtered
through leaves and branches
of dogwood. See bottoms
of droopy green leaves,
hidden, less than perfect,
hardly ever seen.

Listen to bluebirds, shallow breezes,
sounds of leaf meeting leaf.

Let the hammock rock
you into monotony,
drop your mind down to earth,
find a place where thoughts
have not yet formed.

Love and Adore

A dog like that follows you anywhere
barks at strangers, not old friends
digs up voles, clears pests from the garden,
leaves holes all over the yard.

A dog like that runs free,
insists on your company for daily walks
races two miles with ease, then struggles
her way up the staircase when lightening threats,
stays near you, protects you

and sits by the fire when it's cold outside,
basks in green grass when sun shines warm
shows you the way to rest between chores,
never misses performance of butterflies and birds.

Live Today

Do not assault the morning
with vacuums and noise
of sweepers and washers.

Do not hurry to make the bed,
pick up socks, fold laundry
or file papers in alphabetical order.

Leave mowers and blowers till later.
Let telephone, email and television wait.

Listen well to birdsong.
Hear its music for the first time.
Watch the sun come up over the mountain.

Motherless

I

The motherless child
drinks from the nearest cup,
glows with the glimmer
of every touch from passers-by,
accepts bread and wine from anyone,
ignores deep seeds of lonely
while a horn of plenty passes
among a crowd,
dances with all who take her hand,
walks familiar steps
to the corner of a wood,
cries alone.

II

The moon is full.
Sleep hides across the mountain.
I wait for the man to come home.

I walk, feel each blade
of grass beneath bare feet,
smell each laurel blossom,
count every firefly.

Finally I lie down
in the cold field.
Eyes toward heaven,
I give myself to the ground.
The earth responds.

Wedding Toast

We live close to the earth.
The ways of nature teach us in steady
and often surprising ways.
So my wish for you, as you walk this world together:

May the sun shine steady on your path.
May the weeds you pull make space
for seeds only you can sow.
May you hold your own course
as the winds of change blow soft or sharp.

Allow stars and moon to guide your steps.
Look with your third eye.
Listen for bird calls.

Drink from the cleanest brook.
Ground yourselves in truth and curiosity.
Keep the home fires burning.

Let yourselves grow close enough to see
what even the mirror does not reveal.

Perfect Rhythm

Broad wing span, well-muscled,
reddish brown color,
he is quiet in his vigil
until the pierce of his sudden shrill cry
belts sharply across the open field.
He cocks his head, betrays his mood.

Could his warbles and wails be the blues?
Noble, on a wire, waiting to swoop down for a snack,
his eyes miss nothing.
He knows his place. He knows he rules.

In praise, joy, or blues, he flies
with grace and ease through the wind.

Years this red shouldered hawk and I watch each other
as he soars his domain.
I hold the title. He owns the field.

Manifesto

My body knew
before my mind
made thoughts,
before my voice
found words.

Make peace with loss.
Make friends with change.

A candle flickers.
Blue light drowns
by its own flame.
Secret shards
of hope surrender.

Let me live
where crystal clear creeks
slither over small stones,
ripple over rugged rocks,
slide through the smooth,
and rain and tears are welcome
as sunlight and laughter.

Where birth and death
run the same river bed,
I run my life.

Pure Gold

Six o'clock alarm,
pull weeds and till garden
before mid-day heat.

Trip to town, tote
bags of mulch, milk and bread.
Cool dip in fish pond,
minnows nibble toes.

Shade tree, iced tea, good book,
siesta.

Evening chores: pick berries,
mow, mulch newly weeded asparagus bed.

All day my mind rebels,
distracted by leaky refrigerator, price of gas,
pests in my blueberries, people in trouble,
war in the world, poison ivy.

Finally I slip out of gear,
dark dirt takes me down.
Layer by layer I submit,
as I would to no human being.
Layers of truth, lies, wishes and repentance
turn in soil, simple spade, easy dig.

Finally, near the bottom layer of soil,
alone and waiting to be found, fondled, fed,
sits my misplaced sanity.
I slip it on, like a golden gown
over my old work clothes.
Perfect fit.

Four feet away, above ground,
neglected for lack of time,
Stella de Oro grows almost wild.

About the Author

Mary Ricketson, Murphy NC, has been writing poetry 20 years. She is inspired by nature and her work as a mental health counselor. Her poetry has been published in *Wild Goose Poetry Review, Future Cycle Press, Journal of Kentucky Studies, Lights in the Mountains, Echoes Across the Blue Ridge, Red Fox Run, It's All Relative, Old Mountain Press, Whispers*, and her chapbook *I Hear the River Call my Name,* and a full-length collection of poetry, *Hanging Dog Creek,* published by Future Cycle Press.

Currently Mary is using her own poetry to present empowerment workshops, combining roles as writer and her helping role as a therapist. Mary Ricketson's poems and activities relate with nature, facilitate talk about a personal path and focus on growth in ordinary and unusual times.

She is Cherokee County representative to North Carolina Writers Network West, and president of Ridgeline Literary Alliance. She won first place in the 2011 Joyce Kilmer Memorial Forest 75th anniversary national poetry contest. She writes a monthly column, Women to Women, for *The Cherokee Scout.* She is a Certified Clinical Mental Health Counselor and an organic blueberry farmer.